MY
Mindful
LIFE

MY
Mindful
LIFE

Activities for greater
PEACE, CONTENTMENT, and FULFILLMENT

Anna Black

CICO BOOKS

LONDON NEW YORK

Published in 2019 by CICO Books

An imprint of Ryland Peters & Small Ltd

341 E 116th St

New York, NY 10029

www.rylandpeters.com

10 9 8 7 6 5 4 3 2 1

A CIP catalog record for this book is available from the Library
of Congress.

ISBN: 978 1 78249 786 8

Printed in China

Editor: Rebecca Smith

Illustrator: Amy-Louise Evans

Commissioning editor: Kristine Pidkameny

In-house editor: Dawn Bates

Designer: Eliana Holder

Art director: Sally Powell

Production manager: Gordana Simakovic

Publishing manager: Penny Craig

Publisher: Cindy Richards

contents

making the most of this book

Whether you are brand new to mindfulness or practice regularly, the best way to approach it is as an experiment. Let go of any expectations and just see what happens.

In the first section of this book, you'll find background information about mindfulness and some suggestions on how best to approach your practice.

You can then pick and choose practices and activities from the Noticing and Cultivating sections. Sometimes I suggest you do one before another, but there will be page references to help you organize that.

The Challenges section is an opportunity for you to play with setting yourself a goal to practice in a certain way for a period of time. The length of the challenges ranges from 5–21 days, and there's room to create your own. There is also an outline for you to create your own personal retreat—a time of silence, practice, and reflection to deepen your practice.

The final section is the place to list your own resources and make use of some that are provided for you.

Be curious, play, and enjoy the journey!

what is mindfulness?

Mindfulness is simply paying attention. Noticing your experience (thoughts, emotions, sensations) as it arises with curiosity and kindness and without judging it.

We know that we can improve our physical fitness and well-being by exercising regularly, eating our five a day, and drinking plenty of water, but may forget that we have the same capacity to strengthen our mental fitness. Practicing mindfulness meditation can help us do this.

Mindfulness is a trait inherent in all of us, but one that can become obscured. We can cultivate mindfulness and build it up by practicing mindfulness meditation formally and informally (see pages 10–14).

WHERE DOES IT COME FROM?

Mindfulness has been around for thousands of years—its origins lie in Buddhism. This secular form was developed more than 30 years ago by Dr Jon Kabat-Zinn and his colleagues at the Massachusetts General Hospital as a way of helping patients with chronic health conditions. Patients who practiced mindfulness reported a reduction in symptoms and found it easier to handle stress and difficult emotions, plus they experienced a renewed sense of joy in life and a feeling of being more connected with others. There were physiological benefits, too (see page 9). Since then, mindfulness-based approaches to health have been successfully used for many different clinical conditions, including anxiety and depression.

Mindfulness has now moved into the mainstream and has been adapted for use in the workplace, education, sports, prisons, government, and even the US Marines.

how does mindfulness help?

Mindfulness benefits us in many ways, not least by teaching us to relate differently to our experiences—particularly those that are more challenging. We become stressed because we believe that whatever is happening is beyond our mental and physical resources. If how we think about something determines our response to it, then it follows that if we can change the way we think about something, our response will also change. Mindfulness helps us to do that.

Practicing mindfulness changes our perception. Mindfulness meditation helps us develop the capacity to step back and be aware of our thoughts. We learn to see the "stories" that we tell ourselves as narrative rather than fact, and we understand that our thoughts are influenced by our mood—so if we feel happy, we will think more positively about the same event than if we feel anxious or depressed.

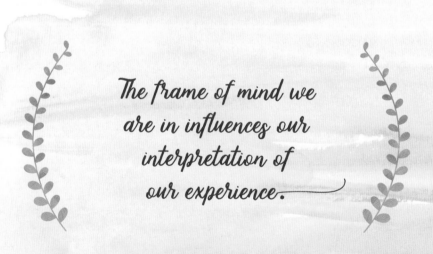

The frame of mind we are in influences our interpretation of our experience.

Once we are aware that we are creating additional layers of suffering by the tales we spin about our experience, we realize we have the ability to let it go. Learning how to do this takes time and practice.

Mindfulness also helps to cultivate an awareness of physical sensations in the body. The mind/body connection is strong and what we are feeling emotionally can manifest in the body. When we are ill or injured, our body also lets us know. However, many of us have become disconnected from the body's physical sensations, not noticing what our bodies are trying to tell us. If we tune in and become aware of our physical self, it will have plenty of feedback for us. This is an important element of mindfulness practice and one of the first things we cultivate.

WIDE-RANGING BENEFITS

One of the main reasons for mindfulness being so widely adopted is its evidence base. Practitioners report benefits such as:

Stress reduction • Increased self-compassion

Better relationships • Improved sleep

Increased happiness • Reduction in symptoms such as pain

Reduced anxiety • More connection with life

Research shows that those people taking an 8-week mindfulness-based stress-reduction course actually changed their brain. Studies have illustrated an increase in activity in areas of the brain that are linked to decision-making, concentration, compassion, empathy, and perspective.

Regular meditation practice also appears to result in a reduction in activity of the amygdala in the brain—the body's in-built alarm system for threat, activated by stress.

how to practice mindfulness

We can practice mindfulness formally or informally. Our aim is simply to be with whatever is arising in that moment of noticing.

FORMAL PRACTICE

This is meditation, which means taking time out to do a form of sitting, lying down, or movement practice for a period of time.

This practice encourages us to show up, regardless of whether we are in the mood or not, and choose a particular focus for attention, such as the breath, physical sensations, thoughts, or sounds. Regular practice cultivates grit—the ability to just do it, even when you would rather not. When the mind wanders—which it will do an awful lot—the invitation is always to notice it has drifted and gently escort the attention back to the focus. Rather than a hindrance, a busy mind is an opportunity to deepen our practice.

Notice WHEN the mind wanders.
Notice WHERE it has gone.
LET GO of the distraction.
Guide the attention back with KINDNESS AND GENTLENESS.
RE-FOCUS the attention on to your chosen point.

The more times we do this, the stronger the new neural pathways in the brain will become. To try some guided meditation practices, go to page 143 for links to free resources.

INFORMAL PRACTICE

This means knowing what you are doing while you are doing it. That is, if you are drinking a cup of tea, drink the tea: inhale the scent, feel the heat of the liquid as it touches the lips, and notice what it feels like as it enters the body. Be with the experience fully. The alternative is to drink the tea while thinking of your to-do list or the argument you had with your partner and, as a result, having no awareness of the experience.

Of course, your world is not going to end if you drink a cup of tea on autopilot, but the danger is that mindlessness can become our default way of living. A life lived without awareness is a bit like sleepwalking through the days, months, and years.

Mindfulness is not a quick fix – it requires regular practice to experience the benefits.

THE VALUE OF BOTH TYPES OF PRACTICE

Informal practices are sometimes seen as having less value than formal meditation, but both are important. Research into the benefits gained from informal practice as opposed to just formal practice is in its infancy, but there are indications that both types give us different things.

Formal

Meditation will bring up all our different mind states: boredom, frustration, anger, restlessness, fear, joy, calm. This gives us an opportunity to practice being with them in a safe space.

Meditating provides the opportunity to sit quietly, just being rather than doing.

Meditating regularly strengthens our commitment to showing up, regardless of the mood we are in.

It's easy to compartmentalize our practice. We can sit in meditation for 20-30 minutes in a quiet room and feel pleased with ourselves for staying calm and non-reactive and yet once we are out in the "real world," we drop back into our default-reacting without awareness.

Informal

It can be hard to find the time to meditate regularly, leading to a feeling of failure. Practicing informally can be easier to fit in, so you can continue to practice.

Informal practices provide an opportunity to learn to weave mindfulness into our day; to live a life with awareness. Our life becomes our practice rather than something separate.

The challenges with informal practice are:

1. Choosing what to do—the opportunities are endless, so we get overwhelmed and do nothing.
2. Remembering to do it. We get caught up in our day.
3. We don't take the time to reflect on what we are learning from it.

In this book, the emphasis is on practicing weaving mindfulness into everyday life with informal practices, although I would encourage you to meditate formally when you can, too, even if only for short periods.

EACH MOMENT IS AN OPPORTUNITY TO *wake up* AND *notice what is arising.*

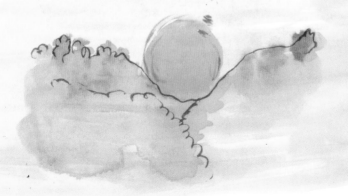

HOW TO PRACTICE INFORMALLY

You can practice mindfulness anywhere, any time, and no one else need know you are doing it. This is very empowering. If you are feeling anxious—perhaps waiting for test results at the doctors—tuning into your experience will shift you from an avoidance mode of mind to one of approach (see page 35). Do this by tuning into your:

HEAD Notice the story you are telling yourself ("If the test result is something bad, I might not be able to work, then I won't be able to pay the mortgage, we'll get evicted..." and before you know it, you'll be mentally squashing you and the kids into one room, living with the in-laws, and you'll have had to get rid of the dog!).

HEART Name any emotions you are aware of—for example, fear.

BODY Be interested about what is happening in the body—what does that emotion feel like physically? Perhaps it's a churning in the stomach, a tightening in the shoulders, rapid breathing. It will be different for each of us and perhaps different every time. Notice how it changes as your thoughts and emotions shift.

Sometimes we may choose to tune into one of these three elements at a time or a combination of them. The key is turning toward our experience with a spirit of friendly interest and acknowledging what is there (even if we don't like it and wish it wasn't).

Jon Kabat-Zinn talks about practice being like weaving a parachute— we develop the skills when we are feeling well, so that when life throws us a curveball we already have the experience to handle it. While we may still find the situation difficult, our landing is softer than it might have been.

WE *can't* STOP
challenging THINGS
HAPPENING TO US, BUT WE
can learn TO
RESPOND *wisely*
RATHER THAN REACT
automatically
TO THEM.

HOW TO APPROACH YOUR PRACTICE

The best way to approach your mindfulness practice is as an experiment—with yourself as the subject. Bear in mind the following:

Try not to have pre-conceived ideas about the outcome, but instead be open to whatever arises.

Be curious and interested in the process itself, rather than fixated on the outcome.

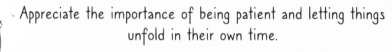

Appreciate the importance of being patient and letting things unfold in their own time.

Reflect on what you notice without judging it.

It's crucial that we don't judge what we notice about our experience and instead cultivate an attitude of friendly curiosity and kindness. There are practices and exercises throughout this book that will encourage you to reinforce these attitudes.

"YOU DON'T HAVE TO ENJOY IT—
just do it"

JON KABAT-ZINN

WEAVING MINDFULNESS INTO YOUR DAY

This three-step approach will help you with your informal practice:

Step 1
SET AN INTENTION to focus on just one thing.

Step 2
SCHEDULE IT... and do it the moment you realize you've forgotten or at the earliest opportunity.

Step 3
REFLECT on what you notice.

Stay focused

Be clear about your intention and it will strengthen your motivation (see page 24).

Be realistic about what is going on in your life and choose practices that are achievable.

Focus on one practice or activity at a time to prevent becoming overwhelmed. Do that one thing for several days.

Tag an activity or practice to something you are already doing (for example, cooking, commuting)—this will create a mental association that will help you to remember, and make you realize when you have forgotten (which will happen frequently).

Reflect on what you notice, to develop insight and learning (see page 18).

the importance of reflection

Taking a moment to reflect on our experience can be a helpful way to draw insights from the practice. We can do this by reviewing in our mind (see How To Practice Mindfulness, page 10) or we can write down some notes. Keeping brief notes is a useful way of noticing patterns that may only become apparent over a period of time.

What you might record in a journal:

What your practice is.

When you did it.

How long for.

What you observed during the practice.

What you noticed after the practice/for the remainder of the day.

It can be helpful to write down what your intentions are for your week's practice—including what you hope to do and when, being as specific as you can.

If you intend to practice but find you keep forgetting, then make the struggle to practice your practice. What is getting in the way? Are you aware of what stops you? If not, practice bringing that into your awareness.

exploring my "why"

You may have many competing demands on your time, so it is important to have a clear understanding of why you want to develop and strengthen your mindfulness practice. Without an overarching vision, your motivation is likely to fade away as other things take priority.

These practices are about exploring what is important to you. What are the guiding principles you would like to live by? Bringing these into awareness means they come into focus—like your very own North Star lighting your path.

It's good to revisit these practices periodically and update them as necessary.

EXPLORING YOUR "WHY"
-WHAT IS IMPORTANT TO YOU
AND WHAT PRINCIPLES
YOU LIKE TO LIVE BY-
IS A WAY OF CONNECTING
TO YOUR PERSONAL VALUES
AND ONE THAT WILL GUIDE
AND STRENGTHEN
YOUR PRACTICE.

what is important to me?

Drawing on what you discovered in the previous practice, write a few words encapsulating your vision of the life you want to lead. This isn't about material things, but rather the qualities you would like to be present. Articulating your vision will strengthen it.

Write it in the present tense and in a positive voice. As well as writing it here, you may want to type it on your computer so that you can print it out and refer to it easily, day to day.

If it feels like anything needs adjusting, edit it from time to time.

MY VISION

harnessing the power of intention

Our intentions drive our thoughts and actions. Much of the time, we are unaware of this and of the potential power that can be harnessed from setting good intentions. Setting a practice plan helps you remember to do it. It reminds you to show up even when you don't really want to.

YOUR GUIDING STAR

If you have done the practice on page 21 ,you will have uncovered what drives and motivates you. It is important to have a sense of this bigger picture, which we can draw on to motivate our practice. Without this, it can be a struggle to keep going. It is one thing to be present with the positive things in our life, but much harder to learn to be with the more challenging aspects, yet that is often where we learn and grow.

When struggling with practicing, you can remind yourself of why you are doing this—and often that the long-term benefit far outweighs the short-term benefit of what is enticing us away.

WHEN YOU MEDITATE

It's helpful to be clear about what your intention is at the very start of your meditation—where you are placing your attention, as well as a reminder of any particular attitudes you want to cultivate.

IN EVERYDAY LIFE

Experiment with exploring intention and how you can bring it into awareness and what happens when you do.

You can set a daily intention, which might be about a particular attitude ("to be kind to myself") or perhaps an action ("to be present with others").

You could create a prompt of some kind as a reminder, but simply setting the intention means at some point in the day, even if we haven't been doing it, we are likely to remember—that is always the opportunity to put it into practice.

You can be intentional about your motivation when speaking to another. Are you trying to score a point or speaking from a place of kindness? The underlying intention will influence your delivery.

How else could you put this into practice in your day?

PAYING ATTENTION
transforms
OUR EXPERIENCE.

noticing

When we pay attention and focus on just one thing at a time, we notice things. Our senses become heightened. We begin to see how patterns of behavior might be linked to the mood we are in, the story we are telling ourselves, or how we are feeling physically.

We become aware of our environment and how it impacts on us both positively and negatively. We discover things about how we interact and respond to other people. We notice what is helpful and what is unhelpful and we can start making conscious choices about how we respond rather than reacting automatically. We can't do anything differently until we become aware of this.

Whenever you are paying attention to your experience, it is important to let go of any expectations about what you will discover. When you do notice something you don't like, be kind to yourself rather than judgmental or self-critical. In order to prevent overwhelm, choose just one activity or practice to do in a given day.

noticing the breath

Our breathing sometimes goes unnoticed, yet it can give us an insight into how we are feeling. When we are anxious or stressed, our breath is usually faster and more shallow; we may even hold it at times. When we are relaxed, we usually breathe more deeply and slowly.

The breath is always there, so it is a great focus for our attention and we can tune into it periodically throughout the day. The more often we do so, the more natural it will become. This practice is simply about noticing the breath and becoming familiar with your breathing patterns.

Tuning in to your breath

Where do you feel the physical sensations of breathing most strongly? It might be in the chest, the belly, or around the nostrils. It doesn't matter where it is—just become familiar with tuning in.

What does your "normal" pattern of breathing feel like?

When you are stressed or anxious, how does your breath change?

How is your breath when you are relaxed?

If you find it hard to connect with the physical sensations of breathing, place your hand on your belly or chest, or at your collarbone. Feel how your body responds to the breath rising and falling.

There is no need to try to breathe in any particular way. The breath doesn't need intervention to do its thing! You are simply practicing tuning in to your breath and gathering information.

REFLECT ON WHAT YOU NOTICE

noticing the body

Often, we don't pay attention to our body until it lets us down and we realize the impact of one part not working as it should.

Practice noticing the following:

POSTURE How are you standing or sitting? Where is your center of gravity? What is happening with the back and shoulders? If you are slouching, how does that impact on your frame of mind and how does it feel physically? Imagine a thread running from the base of the spine, along the back of the neck, and out of the crown of the head. What does it feel like if you pull gently on the imaginary thread?

PHYSICAL SENSATIONS What external and internal sensations do you notice? Where are they? What do they feel like? Are they changing? Notice, too, how you relate to these sensations—is there any felt sense of liking or not liking?

THE BODY IN RELATION TO THE ENVIRONMENT How does it react? Think about temperature, noise, surfaces, smells, and sights.

THE BODY IN RELATION TO OTHERS How does it react to people— those you like, and those you don't? How about strangers? Where in the body do you notice your response? Explore the felt sensations experienced when you interact with someone you love compared to someone who you don't get on with.

THE BODY AND EMOTIONS How does it feel in the body when you are happy, excited, stressed, or anxious? See if you can identify where in the body you experience the sensations and what they feel like.

WHY TUNE INTO THE BODY?

Tuning into the body and its physical sensations is a great way to get out of the head and thoughts of the past (which we can't change) and the future (which is fantasy). Sensations are always shifting and changing, so they can help bring us into the present moment.

Felt sensations are a useful anchor that can ground us in the present moment. Tuning in to the sensation of the feet in contact with the floor is particularly grounding. Try any other touch points, too, such as buttocks on the seat and hands in the lap. Practice doing this as often as you can.

Connecting with the felt sensation of an emotion can help us be with it, which can be a more useful way of processing it than trying to problem-solve it away.

The more we can become familiar with how our body responds and reacts, the more likely we are to pick up helpful warning signs when things go wrong.

REFLECT

Remember it's just an experiment—explore, notice, and reflect on your experience.

check your energy gauge

If you drive a car, you know the importance of checking the gas gauge periodically. The last thing you want is to be left stranded with an empty tank! We each have our own internal "gas" tank: our overall energy that we can keep topped up by eating healthily, getting enough sleep and exercise, doing things that we enjoy, and so on.

Being able to tune into our energy and noticing when it feels depleted is important. We can then take action and decide what we need—perhaps something to eat, a nap, some fresh air. What nourishes and restores our energy will be different for each of us and depends on the circumstances. Sometimes we may need something that energizes us, that gets us up and moving even if we just want to sleep and zone out; other times we may need something more nurturing. Learning to become familiar with your body's needs is essential for self-care.

This practice is a way of tuning in and exploring how you are feeling in this moment. The more regularly you do it, the easier you will find it to pick up early indications from the mind/body that you are under the weather. It is far better to keep your "gas" topped up than enter the red and be running on empty.

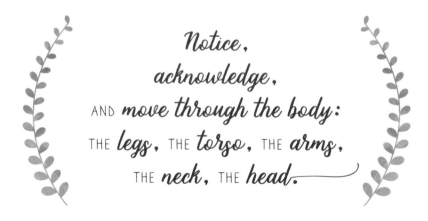

Notice,
acknowledge,
AND move through the body:
THE legs, THE torso, THE arms,
THE neck, THE head.

PRACTICE

Do this periodically over a series of days, perhaps experimenting with different times of day. You may begin to get a sense of any patterns and how certain activities, environments, and people affect you. You are just checking in and seeing how you are, even if you wish it were different.

Take a moment to become aware of the whole body, noticing any touch points where the body is in contact with something else.

Drop your attention to the soles of the feet. Notice any points of contact: weight, pressure, warmth, coolness, air, tingling, itching... What is present?

Begin to move your attention up from the soles of the feet, through the top of the feet, the ankles, the lower legs...

As you shift your attention up and through the body, just notice how you are feeling, becoming aware of any twinges, aches, pains, and noticing any areas of tension or tightness. Or perhaps becoming aware of a fizz of energy, prickles of excitement—an internal buzz. Whatever is present is already here. It is just how you are right now.

Move slowly, lingering in some places as you explore the physical sensations, or you can keep it short, a quick check-in and acknowledgment of how you are. Experiment with both.

Once you've scanned the entire body, ask yourself silently, "How am I feeling right now? How is my energy level?" You can ask yourself this question (or a variation of it) a couple of times. See overleaf for ways to record your observations.

REFLECT

Visualizing the body as an empty container and your energy as a liquid, ask yourself where it would come up to. If your energy is low, it may be down in the lower extremities or you may be brimming with energy up to the crown of the head. Take a moment to acknowledge how you are feeling.

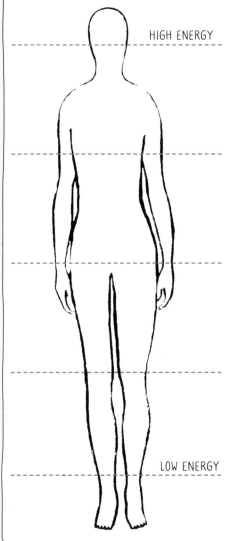

HIGH ENERGY

LOW ENERGY

If you are feeling very depleted, perhaps ask yourself, "What do I need right now? How best can I take care of myself?" Depending on where you are, you may need to modify these needs or park them until a time you can act on them, but remember that small actions can create quite sizeable effects. There may be something you can do right now. You can refer to your list of What Nourishes Me on page 46.

Finish by becoming aware of the whole body and any touch points.

Shade in the body diagram to depict what you discovered about your energy levels.

Remember, energy may be physical, mental, emotional, or a combination. Sometimes one may be more dominant than the others.

Acknowledging how things are moves us into an "approach" mode of mind, accepting what is, rather than an "avoidance" mode, where we pretend everything is okay. Resisting our experience uses up a lot of energy and creates unhappiness.

Use the chart to give a rating of 1—10, with 1 being very depleted and 10 feeling very good. Record any patterns you notice regarding ratings and activities/environments.

DATE	TIME OF DAY	OBSERVATIONS AROUND ACTIVITIES/ENVIRONMENT THAT PRECEDED PRACTICE	RATING 1—10 (1 = LOW 10 = HIGH)

change your seat

Are you someone who always likes to sit in the same place? I, for example, given a choice will take a space that is at the side rather than in the middle. There can be good reasons why we fall into these patterns, but they can reinforce our natural tendency to move into autopilot. We know where we are going, so we tune out from the here and now. We also get used to seeing the world through one particular lens. We can shake things up a bit by intentionally choosing to sit or stand somewhere different and see the world from an altered perspective.

First, notice your habitual patterns. Reflect on your typical routines and where you tend to sit when eating at home, dining out, or on your commute, in a class or meeting... Make a note of what you observe:

PRACTICE

Make the intention to sit in a different place.

Mix it up as much as possible and choose a space somewhere new and different.

Notice how it makes you feel in the head, heart, and body. Is it pleasant, unpleasant, or neutral? How does it affect your experience?

How do others react if, for example, it's a regular event and you are suddenly seated in "someone else's space?"

REFLECT

Make a note of what you discover

mindful mouthful

Engaging with the senses is an easy way to be in tune with the present moment, and mindful eating is a great opportunity to explore the whole realm—taste, touch and texture, smell, sounds, and sight.

Much of the time, we might bolt our food, consuming calories without awareness of the experience. When we do this, we often overeat as we are not tuned into the body's cue that we have had enough and we miss out on the whole sensory experience of eating, which nourishes us much more than just physically (assuming it's good food!).

When we are aware of what we are eating, we are more likely to make healthy choices as we want to engage all the senses in a pleasurable experience.

Eating mindfully is simply being present while eating—so putting down your phone or book, and not chatting. It doesn't mean eating more slowly, although that may happen naturally when you start paying attention.

PRACTICE

Focus on your first mouthful, which is when your attention is most engaged. If you are eating with family and friends, no one need know you are doing it.

You might notice:

HOW THE FOOD LOOKS: colors, shapes, surfaces.

THE SCENT: what can you detect?

THE TEXTURE: how does it feel in your hand or mouth?

THE TASTE: does the taste hit you in one blast or build up slowly? Maybe something kicks in a bit later.

ANY SOUNDS: does it crunch, crackle, or pop?

There's no need to think too much about it. Be alive to your own response—what you like or don't like, or what you tune out from.

Is there an accompanying narrative—memories, associations, thoughts?

Perhaps there's an emotional response. Maybe you notice physical sensations in the body, which arise in response to the senses, the thoughts, or the emotions?

Simply be present. Be open to whatever arises.

If you'd like to explore the senses some more, check out the 5 Days 5 Senses Challenge on page 106.

what pushes your stress buttons?

Becoming familiar with your response to stress is important as being able to pick up on the early warning signs means you can take action before things spiral out of control. We can't make changes until we are aware of what is happening for us.

It's helpful to understand:

What makes you stressed—what are your triggers?

How do you feel physically in the body when you are stressed?

How does it affect your behavior?

Start noticing these things—it is easier if you choose to focus on them one at a time, but if you have other observations as well, just gather information as you discover it. It might be something that you come back to over a period of time.

LEARNING FROM YOUR BODY

Many of us can feel quite disconnected from our bodies—maybe we live mostly in our heads or we have a difficult relationship with our body. Perhaps we feel it is letting us down as we age, gives us pain, or maybe it doesn't look as we would like it to. We can redress this by regularly tuning into the body (see page 30). The more we do this, the easier it will be to pick up on physical sensations as they arise.

WHAT MAKES YOU STRESSED?

Record anything you notice that causes you stress—it might be particular people or events, or an environment. Try to be as specific as possible, so rather than writing "work," try to pinpoint what it is specifically at work that makes you stressed, for example, "someone asking me to do something last minute."

HOW DO YOU FEEL PHYSICALLY
WHEN YOU ARE STRESSED?

Start tuning into the body when you are stressed and see what you notice. Some people may feel sick or find their body tenses or they get sweaty palms. Just jot down anything and everything you observe. When you are stressed, it may be that there are physical sensations that happen in the moment (such as sweaty palms) and those that arise later (such as headaches).

....

....

....

....

....

HOW DOES YOUR BEHAVIOR CHANGE
WHEN YOU ARE STRESSED?

We all react in different ways when stressed. You may eat more or less— or be more likely to reach for a sweet treat. Your sleep or interactions with others might be affected. Just notice whatever comes up for you.

....

....

....

....

WHETHER WE FEEL SOMETHING IS *stressful* OR NOT DEPENDS ON HOW WE *perceive it*.

IF WE VIEW IT AS SOMETHING THAT *threatens* OUR WELL-BEING, THEN IT BECOMES A *stressor*.

IF WE CAN CHANGE OUR *perception* OF IT, THEN IT WON'T FEEL SO *stressful*.

PRACTICE

In the table below, make a list of five things that are making you anxious or stressed at the moment. You don't have to fill the table—just list what comes to mind, being as specific as you can.

In column two, rate each item on a scale of 1—10, with 1 being not stressful and 10 being very stressful, and enter the date.

Once you have made your list, take a moment to reflect on the experience. What comes up for you? Make a note opposite.

After a period of four weeks or so, come back to the list and review it. Rate them again and add a date. Take a moment to reflect on any changes. What is different, if anything? Make a note opposite.

When you come to review, you may find that there are new things now in your top stressors, so you can add these and start the process again.

DESCRIPTION	ORIGINAL DATE AND RATING	LATER DATE AND REVISED RATING
1.		
2.		
3.		
4.		
5.		

OBSERVATIONS

what nourishes me?

Noticing what nourishes you physically, mentally, and emotionally can be a helpful way to build up a collection of self-care strategies you can use regularly to maintain your well-being and also to draw on in times of distress.

Give each activity a star rating, but remember not all need to be five stars. Sometimes just a little attention and kindness to ourselves can make us feel better. Small shifts can make a big difference.

You may want to create this list over a period of time as you observe what you find works well. Try to be as specific as you can—for example, if there is a particular type of music or artist you find nourishing, jot it down.

Some ideas:

Physical exercise, crafting, baking, learning a skill, taking a bath, socializing, eating favorite foods, talking to a friend, reading a book, listening to music, spending time with family, helping someone else, gardening, taking a day trip.

ACTIVITY	TIME NEEDED	HOW IT MAKES ME FEEL?	COST
		☆ ☆ ☆ ☆ ☆	☆ ☆ ☆ ☆
		☆ ☆ ☆ ☆ ☆	☆ ☆ ☆ ☆ ☆
		☆ ☆ ☆ ☆ ☆	☆ ☆ ☆ ☆ ☆
		☆ ☆ ☆ ☆ ☆	☆ ☆ ☆ ☆ ☆
		☆ ☆ ☆ ☆ ☆	☆ ☆ ☆ ☆ ☆
		☆ ☆ ☆ ☆ ☆	☆ ☆ ☆ ☆ ☆
		☆ ☆ ☆ ☆ ☆	☆ ☆ ☆ ☆ ☆
		☆ ☆ ☆ ☆ ☆	☆ ☆ ☆ ☆ ☆
		☆ ☆ ☆ ☆ ☆	☆ ☆ ☆ ☆ ☆
		☆ ☆ ☆ ☆ ☆	☆ ☆ ☆ ☆ ☆
		☆ ☆ ☆ ☆ ☆	☆ ☆ ☆ ☆ ☆
		☆ ☆ ☆ ☆ ☆	☆ ☆ ☆ ☆ ☆

Once you've created a number of items on your list, you can create your own Self-Care Menu on page 70.

how am I right now?

Checking in with yourself periodically throughout your day and acknowledging how you are feeling is a great practice. Begin by setting an intention to do it, say, three times a day and although you will probably forget, at some point you will remember and that's the time to do the check in. Over time, you will find yourself just doing it without thinking about it.

EACH MOMENT
IS AN OPPORTUNITY TO
wake up AND *notice*
what is arising.

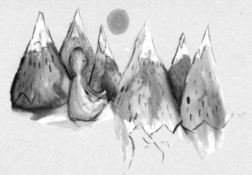

PRACTICE

The initial acknowledgment step is particularly important,
so don't skip it.

Step 1: Acknowledge

Check in with yourself. Ask yourself, "How am I right now?" (or a similar phrase). Notice if there is a particular story or thought in your head, and acknowledge any emotions or physical sensations in the body. Sometimes you may be aware of all three categories, other times just one or a couple. That's okay. This step is a quick check-in to simply acknowledge how you are and what you are experiencing— even if you don't like it or don't think you should be feeling that way.

Step 2: Breathe

Take your attention to the breath. If it's helpful, repeat silently to yourself: "In/Out."

Do this a few times.

Step 3: Expand

Widen your attention out from your breath, noticing the body, particularly any touch points (feet on the floor, buttocks on the seat, and so on), sounds, and the environment around you.

Continue with your day.

For tips to help you remember to do the practice, see page 17.

hold the front page

Nowadays, with 24-hour news stations providing an endless diet of drama and tragedy, world events can feel draining to watch. You can limit your own exposure to it, but if it's still taking its toll on your energy levels or mood, you can shift the focus toward noticing what is positive in your own life.

If you were to put together a front page of events that you would like to acknowledge and celebrate, those that have happened to family, friends, colleagues, and neighbors, what would you include?

Focus on small, everyday events and experiences that made you or the person feel good.

It might be something that someone has done for another person: perhaps you picked the first and only tomato you've grown this year; maybe you stopped to listen to a bird sing. Perhaps a friend received some good news, or a son or daughter lost a tooth...

CREATE YOUR OWN "FRONT PAGE" OF GOOD NEWS OVER A PERIOD
OF TIME, ADDING TO IT AS YOU GO ALONG.

noticing a typical day

Reflecting on how you perceive the different activities you regularly undertake can give useful feedback.

Step 1

Make a list of activities you do in a typical day. Break down chunks of time into tasks, where possible, and be as specific as you can.

Step 2

Go back over your list and, using the key opposite, rate each activity.

Step 3

What do you notice? Any surprises or patterns?

Step 4

Revisit your list. Is there anything you could do differently to make a neutral activity more positive and a negative one at least neutral? Can you weave in more of the positive occurrences into your day?

You may want to experiment with bringing a different attitude to particular activities or simply paying attention to how it feels physically and emotionally. If you do something with a feeling of resentment, for example, that will feel very different to choosing to do it with good grace since you know it has to be done.

Is there something you could do before or after an undertaking that might affect it? Acknowledging that something is difficult and challenging can be helpful and then we can decide what we could do as a counter-balance to take care of ourselves (see page 70).

Key

+ POSITIVE / ENJOYABLE / NOURISHING
X NEGATIVE / STRESSFUL / DEPLETING
_ NEUTRAL / NEITHER ONE THING OR THE OTHER

☐
☐
☐
☐
☐
☐
☐
☐

REFLECTION

WHAT COULD YOU DO DIFFERENTLY?

how do you listen?

This practice is all about noticing the typical patterns you fall into when interacting with others. Often we discover that, rather than listening to what someone is saying to us, we are thinking of something else, rehearsing what we are going to say in response, or jumping in with a "me too" story. Sometimes we mask our own discomfort by trying to make the other person's pain go away or to fix their problem.

Try this..

Make a daily intention to notice how you listen.

Ideally, do this over a period of time—a few days or a week—so you can build up a picture to see if your listening patterns vary with different people and/or locations.

Remember to let go of judging what you notice—all you are doing at this point is noticing your own typical patterns. You can't do anything differently until you develop awareness so this is an important first step in cultivating a new way of listening (see page 92).

Experiment with...

Listening at work, at home, and when you are out and about.

How you listen with different people—co-workers, family members, strangers, people serving you, different age groups.

Do you listen differently in a one-to-one situation compared to in a group?

Noticing how the frame of mind you are in might affect how you listen.

Do this in reverse–notice how it affects you when someone is really present when you are talking, compared to when they are not.

WHAT DID YOU NOTICE? (INCLUDE DETAILS OF WHERE YOU WERE, THE TYPE OF PERSON YOU WERE WITH, YOUR OWN MOOD, PLUS ANY PATTERNS YOU NOTICED).

TYPICAL PATTERNS I FALL INTO
(TICK THOSE THAT YOU'VE NOTICED)

- [ ] Rehearsing
- [ ] "Me too"
- [ ] Fixing
- [ ] Judging self
- [ ] Judging others

- [ ] Mind wandering
- [ ] Multi-tasking
- [ ] Interrupting
- [ ] ....
- [ ] ....

- [ ] ....
- [ ] ....
- [ ] ....
- [ ] ....
- [ ] ....

what are you feeding?

When we start paying attention to our internal experience
(our thoughts, emotions, and physical sensations), we begin to notice
how the way we relate to our experience is influenced by the
"thought story" we tell ourselves. We start to see how we often
"feed" a story by fueling it. Once we become aware of these patterns,
we can bring our attention to the body to ground ourselves (see
page 31) and notice how the "story" manifests physically. By observing
our thoughts in this way, we gain some perspective and can see them
simply as weather, which come and goes according to our mood.

What are the top 5 thought stories current for you right now? Color
in the stars to rank their dominance, with 5 being the most dominant.

.... ☆ ☆ ☆ ☆ ☆

.... ☆ ☆ ☆ ☆ ☆

.... ☆ ☆ ☆ ☆ ☆

.... ☆ ☆ ☆ ☆ ☆

.... ☆ ☆ ☆ ☆ ☆

"*Thoughts* ARE
NOT *facts*–EVEN THE
ONES THAT SAY
THEY ARE."

PROFESSOR
MARK WILLIAMS

How many of these thought patterns do you experience in a typical day?

MIND-READING
"He/she thinks I'm useless."

CATASTROPHIZING
"XYZ is a disaster."

CRYSTAL-BALL GAZING
"I know XYZ is going to happen."

BLAMING (SELF)
"I must have done something wrong."

BLAMING (OTHERS)
"It's so and so's fault, not mine."

ETERNALIZING
"It's never going to change."

PERFECTIONISM
"I/they shouldn't make mistakes."

JUDGING
"I am not good enough; it/they are not good enough."

Practice

Choose the top three stories present for you right now and make those the focus of your attention. Notice how the story manifests itself as a thought and identify what type of thinking it is (you can look at the list on page 57 if you need help identifying it). Make a note of any accompanying physical sensations or emotions that you become aware of (you may want to explore these over a period of time).

Observe, too, whether there are particular circumstances when this story shows up. To lend some perspective, give it a light-hearted nickname so that when you become aware of the story you can label it—for example, "there's the poison parrot sounding off again."

THOUGHT EG "I shouldn't have made a mistake"	TYPE OF THOUGHT EG perfectionism
PHYSICAL SENSATIONS THAT ACCOMPANY THE THOUGHT STORY EG sick feeling in belly	EMOTIONS THAT ACCOMPANY THE THOUGHT STORY EG shame—not good enough
NICKNAME	
WHEN IT SHOWS UP EG at work with my boss	

THOUGHT	TYPE OF THOUGHT

PHYSICAL SENSATIONS THAT ACCOMPANY THE THOUGHT STORY	EMOTIONS THAT ACCOMPANY THE THOUGHT STORY
NICKNAME	
WHEN IT SHOWS UP	

THOUGHT	TYPE OF THOUGHT

PHYSICAL SENSATIONS THAT ACCOMPANY THE THOUGHT STORY	EMOTIONS THAT ACCOMPANY THE THOUGHT STORY
NICKNAME	
WHEN IT SHOWS UP	

how do you relate to your phone?

The benefits of smartphones are huge—we can stay connected with others regardless of where we are, save time by shopping online, have the latest news at our fingertips—but we can also become enslaved by them. Noticing how you relate to your phone can highlight unhelpful patterns that can impact negatively on your well-being.

Observe

How often do you check your phone?

Where are you and what you are doing when you check it?

What mood are you usually in when you become aware of the impulse (bored, stressed, anxious, calm, happy...)?

What you are doing—checking emails (personal or work), social media, shopping, watching videos?

How long do you usually spend on your phone at any time?

How do you feel after being on your phone. Does it nourish you or drain your energy?

Remember you are simply gathering feedback—you would usually do these things unconsciously and so if you can begin to notice the context and the impulse, you can start making more conscious choices. Often it is only minor calibrations that are needed to shift an unhealthy relationship into one that is more balanced.

If you want to explore this practice further, try the Tech Detox challenge on page 100.

WHAT DID YOU NOTICE?

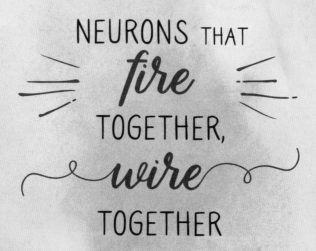

NEURONS THAT *fire* TOGETHER, *wire* TOGETHER

RICK HANSON

NEUROPSYCHOLOGIST AND AUTHOR

cultivating

When we practice mindfulness, we are not intentionally chasing a particular experience. Instead we are practicing being with all our experiences: the good, the bad, and the neutral.

However, one of the benefits of practicing—particularly informally—is that we naturally start doing more of the things that we find helpful and nourishing.

The more we engage in the positive behaviors, the more likely we are to do them more often. Our brain loves repetition, whether it is reinforcing negative or positive behaviors. Therefore we can train our brain and lay down new neural pathways by practicing positive actions such as letting go of distractions, returning to a point of focus, and cultivating kindness and interest.

As well as cultivating positive behaviors, this section is about developing our mindfulness "muscle of awareness," strengthening our skills, and practicing turning toward and being with whatever arises in our life.

grow a little mindfulness

Apart from the physical exercise of gardening, being outside instantly expands our perspective and encourages us to look outward rather than stay stuck in internal over-thinking.

There is much to learn from nature. However freezing and gray winter is, the day will come when we notice a bud breaking, feel the warmth of the wind rather than its chill, and realize that the weather has shifted. The natural world reminds us that everything passes at some point.

Being outdoors is a sensory rollercoaster that can place us right in the present moment: the damp potting compost running through our fingers, the sharp tang of a freshly torn basil leaf, the sweetness of a picked strawberry, the sighing of the wind through the trees...

Gardening is an opportunity to nurture—to plant a seed, care for it as it sprouts, support it as it grows tall, and appreciate its beauty or bounty.

We can benefit from gardening, whether or not we have a garden. Wherever you live, there is always room for a pot on a window sill. Planting seeds is a great opportunity to grow your mindfulness.

TRY THIS

It is great to do this practice with herbs as they are fast-growing, have a strong smell, and can be used as part of a mindful eating or food preparation practice.

Experiment with growing at least one of your herbs from seed. There is something magical about following the cycle from a dry dot to something green, leafy, and bursting with scent and flavor.

Make notes in the space below about the planting, perhaps taking into account the following:

How did you choose what to plant? What was that decision-making process like? What patterns, if any, did you notice?

Notice the sensory experience of planting: the soil on your hands, the dirt under your nails. Was it pleasant? Unpleasant? It doesn't matter which, but simply observe.

Be aware of any stories unfolding in your mind. How far are you projecting forward into the future? Or perhaps you are jumping back into the past and comparing with previous successes or failures. Simply notice and bring yourself back to now.

How did you feel when the seeds were all tucked up in the soil?

Nurturing

Once your seeds are planted, notice whether you are able to let things unfold in their own time or if there is a desire to poke around to see if anything is growing. Are you smothering your plants with attention? How do you feel if you neglect your seedlings?

Planting seeds is like our mindfulness practice—nothing seems to be happening on the surface at first, but there are often things shifting and changing deep inside. It's best to leave alone, water if needed, adjust the temperature or light perhaps, but let things unfold in their own time. Notice any impatience and treat it kindly: "Ah—there I go again—leaning forward, wanting the next things to happen now!"

There is a balance with our practice—cultivating it but not constantly measuring it against some invisible yardstick. This gives us an expectation of where we think it should be and if it falls short, we are disappointed. The wild strawberry may not be as big and juicy as the commercially cultivated one, but it has a sweetness all of its own.

Exploring

Once your seeds have germinated and grown, your practice can shift to exploring the plant via the senses—the smell, the taste of a torn leaf, perhaps the flavor combined with something else... Make a point of using your herb(s) to create flavorsome food. Preparing and eating a freshly made salad topped with herbs, for example, is an opportunity for practice.

DATE:

OBSERVATIONS:

DATE:

OBSERVATIONS:

DATE:

OBSERVATIONS:

DATE:

OBSERVATIONS:

TIPS

Check the seed packet for information on planting depth, seed spacing and thinning, germination instructions, and so on.

Label your pots with variety and date of sowing so you know when you should plant some more.

Sow fresh seeds monthly for a steady crop.

take a walk

Getting outside and intentionally tuning into the natural world is a great way to connect with the present moment. We can use our senses to connect with the environment around us.

Find somewhere that has some greenery—a park or open space in the country or by the coast. Make an intention to be present. Leave your phone at home or turn it to silent.

Just walk and be open to whatever arises. You are not looking for anything specific so let go of striving to have a particular experience.

Things you may become aware of:

The weather—are you tensing up against it or basking in it? What do you feel against your skin?

Smells and scents.

Textures, colors, and patterns—on the ground, in the bark, the leaves, the flowers, the sky, the water...

Sounds—animals, insects, airplanes, cars, sirens, talking, laughing...

Finish the sentence below and then continue writing without stopping or reading it back until you reach the end of the page. Start subsequent sentences with: "I noticed..."

ON MY WALK, I NOTICED...

my self-care menu

In What Nourishes Me? on page 70, you created your go-to menu of self-care activities. Try to have a wide range of strategies, from quick and simple to some that require a bit of thought and planning.

Once you have your menu, aim to schedule these into your life—particularly the items that need more planning. This will increase the likelihood of them coming to fruition. Too often, we will give up the things that nourish us first so we don't disappoint or let down other people. This is a mistake.

You need TO TAKE CARE OF *yourself* BEFORE YOU CAN TAKE CARE OF *anyone else.*

DURATION	DESCRIPTION	PREPARATION NEEDED
	1. 2. 3. 4.	
	1. 2. 3. 4.	
	1. 2. 3. 4.	
	1. 2. 3. 4.	

see through the eyes of a friend

Many of us struggle to see ourselves clearly and we can be self-critical, thinking that we should be better than we are.

Try this

Imagine you are one of your really good friends or perhaps a grandparent—someone who loves and cares about you and enjoys your company. Picture this person—hold them in your mind's eye and remember how you feel when you are in their company.

How would they describe you? What does this person say to you when you are feeling down or struggling?

On the facing page, just write whatever arises—there's no need to edit and don't stop until you reach the end of the page. Begin each sentence: You are...

When you are done, take a moment to read back through the words. How do they make you feel? What do you notice?

YOU ARE...

letting go

This is a meditation that you can do quietly at home or, alternatively, while sitting on a bus or train, or at your desk. When we exhale, we are releasing air—letting it go. Noticing how the body responds as we breathe out is the focus of this practice.

Practice

Begin by tuning in to your breathing. Notice where you are feeling the breath most strongly—the chest, belly, or around the upper lip—and make that the focus of your attention.

Once you are aware of the breath, narrow your focus to your out-breath only.

You may still be aware of the in-breath and that's okay—we are simply making our primary focus the out-breath.

Breathing out. Releasing the breath. Letting it go.

If it's helpful you can silently repeat "Out" each time you breathe out.

Continue for as long as you wish.

curiouser and curiouser

When we are curious about something, we are interested, engaged, we want to find out more—there is a sense of excitement about the unexpected. This is very much an "approach" mode of mind (see page 35). Children are endlessly curious about the world. As we get older, we become more jaded by life and adopt a "been there, done that" mentality and tune out from experiences we think we know about. When we do this, we short-change ourselves and miss out on so much.

Cultivate an attitude of curiosity by:
Asking questions—to yourself as well as others—and remaining open to the answers.

Letting go of expectations about how you think something will be and instead intentionally inviting yourself to experience it as it actually is.

Spending time with a child and following their lead—it's infectious!

Be curious about:
Your internal experience • The world around you
• Other people • The natural world • Everything else!

When we practice curiosity, it is with a spirit of friendly interest rather than analysis. We are interested in what is happening rather than why it is happening.

a letter to myself

When we are feeling low, it can be hard to motivate ourselves and remember helpful strategies. This exercise—a letter to yourself that can be read in difficult moments—is a way of gently reminding yourself of what is possible. Write it in the spirit of one friend giving wise advice to another.

Do this exercise when you are feeling good about yourself. Before writing the letter, take a moment to reflect on what you have found helpful in the past to shift a low mood, remembering if there are specific tactics that you have employed.

You might want to remind yourself of any achievements or compliments given to you. There may be specific jokes that are cheering to recall or uplifting stories you want to draw upon—include anything you think might be helpful. You know yourself better than anybody else.

DEAR

turning toward the difficult

There will always be experiences that we don't like and we may have no choice but to put up with them, which can create resistance and suffering. However, we can cultivate a willingness to be with these experiences and practice "turning toward" what we don't like in a way that is safe and non-threatening.

Using food is a good option as we all have food that we don't like because of the texture, smell, taste—or maybe it reminds us of an experience we'd rather forget. It can be interesting to revisit this food— with new goggles of awareness on and with a spirit of turning toward it.

Practice

This is about exploring our reactions and being with something we don't like, so take baby steps and initially choose something that you would prefer not to eat rather than something you dislike intensely. You can build up to something more difficult.

It's important to ground yourself at the start and then periodically throughout the practice. It's a bit like dipping a toe in the water of the experience—and then pulling back from it and bringing our awareness into the body before trying again, if it feels okay to do so.

Don't force yourself to do anything and feel free to stop at any point. It's not about actually eating the item, but rather exploring your reaction to it, and being aware of any expectations you bring to it.

Remember—it's not about having to like the item!

Step 1

Take a moment to ground yourself. Notice the sensations of the soles of the feet on the floor, the buttocks on the chair if you are seated, and any other touch points.

Step 2

Notice your initial response to the item. What do you observe? The smell, the texture, the colors, the shape. What story is playing in your mind? How is your body reacting—do you notice any physical sensations. If so, where are they and what are they like? Are you aware of any emotions present?

Connect with your feet on the floor and any other touch points periodically to ground yourself.

Feel free to stop the practice at any time.

Step 3

If it feels okay, you can pick up the item and explore it a bit more closely—perhaps bring it up to your lips for example—all the time, noticing your response in the head, heart, and body.

Continue to ground yourself and pause or stop at any time.

Step 4

Place the item in your mouth and continue to explore it with awareness. What do you notice? You may choose to end there or continue eating. Record your observations overleaf.

WHAT WAS THE STORY PLAYING IN YOUR MIND? DID IT REMAIN
THE SAME OR CHANGE THROUGH THE EXPERIENCE?

WERE YOU AWARE OF ANY EMOTIONS ARISING? WHAT WERE THEY
AND DID THEY SHOW UP IN THE BODY, IF AT ALL?

WHAT PHYSICAL SENSATIONS DID YOU NOTICE IN THE BODY?
WHERE WERE THEY LOCATED AND HOW WOULD YOU DESCRIBE
THE SENSATION(S)?

WHAT ELSE DID YOU NOTICE ABOUT THE EXPERIENCE? WERE
THERE ANY SURPRISES? HOW DID THE EXPERIENCE DIFFER FROM
YOUR EXPECTATIONS?

simply the breath

Focusing on the breath is my favorite go-to practice. I can do it in any location, when I'm alone or with others; I can do it for a second or two or for an extended period of time. I do it when I'm feeling good, sad, stressed, or angry. It grounds me in the moment and reins in my thoughts.

Practice

These instructions are simple and taught by Buddhist teacher and author, Thich Nhat Hanh:

1. Become aware of your breath.

2. As you breathe in, say to yourself, "Breathing in I know that I'm breathing in."

3. As you breathe out, say to yourself, "Breathing out I know that I'm breathing out."

4. You may find yourself simplifying it to "in" and "out."

That's it. Try it.

Breathe
AND KNOW
THAT YOU ARE
breathing.

drawing blind by touch

A blind touch drawing is liberating. Your eyes are closed so there are no expectations that what you produce is going to look anything like a "good" drawing in the traditional sense. We are using the sense of touch to feel our way across the landscape of the face and that moves us into a different relationship with our features and how we look. The result is a felt self-portrait.

These drawings can be very quick so it can be fun to do several at a time.

You will need:

Several sheets of paper—copier paper is fine. Larger sheets are better, so if you only have A4 (letter size), stick two sheets together (use tape on the reverse) to create a larger sheet.

Drawing implement (such as sharp pencil, felt pen, or charcoal)

Masking tape

Golden rule—no peeking until you come to a natural stop!

Step 1

Tape the paper onto the table so it doesn't move around. Position yourself so you are seated directly in front of the paper and your drawing implement is in your hand.

Step 2

Close your eyes and take a moment or two to connect to the touch points of the body.

Step 3

Raise your non-drawing hand to your face and when you are ready, begin to move one finger slowly across and around the landscape of your features. As you move the non-drawing hand, the drawing hand also moves in time with the other hand, echoing what you are experiencing through touch.

Notice the textures you feel. This may influence the pressure or weight you bring to bear on the drawing tool.

Let go of any thoughts about what you are drawing. You are exploring rather than rendering a likeness.

Go wherever you go without forcing or directing. You may revisit a location, you may traverse a long distance—KEEP YOUR DRAWING IMPLEMENT IN CONTACT WITH THE PAPER AT ALL TIMES.

Feel your way with the finger and the drawing implement simultaneously. Whenever you feel it comes to a natural end, just stop. Often this is because the thinking mind has become too strong and we notice ourselves beginning to direct the drawing or even peeking!

Do the exercise as many times as you like. Experiment with switching the drawing tool to the non-dominant hand.

drawing the breath

Explore a different relationship with your breath. All you will need is a sharp pencil (no need for any special kind) and a piece of paper (standard copier paper is fine).

Seat yourself at a table with the paper in front of you. Hold the pencil so the tip is lightly in contact with the paper. Sit in a balanced position with both feet flat on the floor.

Close your eyes (and no peeking until the end).

Begin to be aware of your breathing. Tuning into its rhythm. No need to change it or direct it in any particular way. As you settle into the breath, allow the pencil to join in. Don't think about the marks, simply move the pencil in response to the sensations of breathing.

No need to control anything. Just let the breath breathe itself and the pencil move with the breath.

Continue until you lose the connection—perhaps your mind wanders or your movements simply come to rest.

Take a moment to pause with your eyes remaining closed. Then open your eyes and look at the marks of your breath.

You can repeat either on the same paper or with a fresh one. If you are working on the same piece of paper, you could use different colored pencils each time.

drawing sound

Sound is a great sense to explore through mark-making. All you will
need is a sharp pencil (no need for any special kind) and a piece of
paper (standard copier paper is fine).

Seat yourself at a table with the paper in front of you.
Hold the pencil so the tip is lightly in contact with the
paper. Sit in a balanced position with both feet flat on the floor.

Keep your eyes closed and don't open them until
you've stopped drawing.

Begin to become aware of your breath. Noticing its rise and fall.
No need to try and change it or direct it in any way. As you settle
into the breath, turn up the dial of awareness to include sounds—both
near and far. The body acts as a receiver picking up any noise.

Just as the body responds to sound, allow the pencil to respond, too.
How does the sound feel—is the rhythm regular or irregular? Is it
soft and light or harsh and loud? Notice if there is a sense of liking
or not liking... invite them all in.

Don't think about the marks being made; simply move the pencil in
response to them. There is no need to control anything. Continue
until you lose the connection—perhaps your mind wanders or your
movements simply come to rest.

Take a moment to pause with your eyes remaining closed. Then open
your eyes and look at the soundscape you've illustrated.

You can repeat either on the same paper or with a fresh piece. If
you are working on the same piece of paper, you could use different
colored pencils each time.

banking the good

Human beings are primed to remember a potential threat, which is why we tend to focus too much on negative experiences and let the positive ones slip away from us. When we are feeling down or stressed, we are also more likely to actively look for evidence to corroborate our "story" and we may dismiss anything that presents a different perspective.

This activity does two things—taking the time to reflect on a positive experience helps us "bank" it in our long-term memory, and having a physical reminder that we can return to helps bring some perspective when we are focused on the negative.

You will need a jar or small box and some scraps of paper and a pen. Keep these out somewhere in sight so it's easy to add to it.

TIPS

Don't skip Step I when you are "paying in." Taking a moment to reflect on the experience will reinforce it in your memory.

Be as specific as you can when describing the experience.

When you've made a "withdrawal," you can always put the memory back in the jar for another time.

Aim to build this appreciation practice into your daily routine.

MAKE AN INVESTMENT

When something positive happens, as soon as possible take a moment to write a brief description of it. An example might be someone pays you a compliment, or you do something you're proud of, or you experience something that makes you feel happy, content, or safe. Be as creative as you like.

Step 1

Pause and bring the experience to mind. Allow yourself to tune in and notice how it makes you feel in the head, heart, and body.

Step 2

Write a line or two about the experience. Fold up the paper and put it in the jar.

Take the time to build up your "investments."

MAKE A WITHDRAWAL

Step 1

When you are feeling down or stressed—or perhaps just make it a weekly ritual—remove one of the folded papers.

Step 2

As you read it, notice what arises for you. What do you feel in the head, heart, and body?

In his book,
The Art of Forgiveness, Loving Kindness, and Peace Buddhist teacher
and author, Jack Kornfield tells the story of
the Babemba tribe in Southern Africa who, when
a member of the tribe behaves irresponsibly or
badly, come together in a circle around the individual.
One by one each member of the tribe recounts
something positive about the person in the center.
When everyone has finished, there is much
celebration as the person is welcomed back
into the family and community.

finding the good

When we are having difficulties in a friendship or relationship, we often focus on the current issue and we can forget about the positive things that have drawn us to that person in the past.

Here we focus on what we have common with the person—highlighting the similarities rather than the differences—and ends with reminding ourselves of three positive things about them.

Practice

Bring to mind someone you are finding tricky at the moment. It might be a family member, a friend, or a co-worker.

Without stopping to edit or think too much, list as many things as you can that you have in common with them. Be as specific as you can.

Next list three positive things about them—again, be as specific as you can and put down whatever comes to you first. It may include how they have behaved with you in the past or perhaps how they are with others. If you can only think of one, that is enough!

cultivating presence with others

If you have done the practice on page 54, you will be familiar with your own listening patterns and also how you feel when someone is or isn't present when you are talking. Being truly heard by another person is a great gift. We can strengthen our ability to be present simply by actively paying attention.

Make an intention to practice mindful listening in a particular environment or with a specific person. We are more likely to remember our intention if we can ring fence it initially rather than try to listen mindfully to everything/everyone. You can experiment with different situations and people over time.

Step 1

Remind yourself of your intention every time you come into the chosen environment or interact with that person. Remove any physical distractions such as your phone.

Step 2

Listen to what is being said. Give the speaker room to speak and pause without interruption.

Step 3

Notice when your attention wanders. Acknowledge your own thoughts and bring the attention back (without judging).

Step 4

When the speaker finishes, pause. Notice and acknowledge whatever may be arising for you in the head, heart, and body. Respond when you are ready—and that response may be a simple "thanks" rather than a comment or solution.

At any point, particularly if you notice yourself reacting, connect with any touch points of the body—the feet on the floor, the buttocks on the seat, the warmth of your hands around a hot drink...

Reflect on how the experience was for you and how it felt compared to your usual mode of listening, plus any feedback you pick up from the other person.

TIPS

Practice this with non-emotionally charged encounters initially.

Remember, we are working with lifetime habits, so learning to do something different will take time.

Be curious—notice if the thought "I know what they are going to say" pops into your mind and instead remain open to what is said.

Be alert to noticing the speaker's non-verbal cues, which you may miss if you are multi-tasking or distracted.

WHAT DID YOU NOTICE?

kindness

How many ways can you express kindness? Think about how you can offer kindness to yourself, your family, friends, co-workers, strangers, the neighborhood, an animal ...

Set an intention to perform at least one act of kindness today. Offer without any expectation of reward. The other person may not even be aware of your act. Notice how it makes you feel. Acts of kindness benefit you too.

For example, you could:

Give up your seat.

Pick up a piece of garbage in the street.

Put some bird food out.

Open the door for someone.

Run an errand for a person who can't.

Phone a friend who is struggling.

Smile at a stranger.

Add some ideas of your own:

....

....

....

....

....

REFLECTION

Notice how it makes you feel in the moment—tune into physical sensations, too—and as you reflect now. You can make this a regular, everyday practice.

cultivating self-compassion

Mindfulness is one of the cornerstones of self-compassion. The Self-Compassion Break, an exercise outlined below and developed by Christopher Germer and Kristin Neff in their Mindful Self-Compassion program, is a terrific practice to do when things feel tough—and we can do it any time, any place, and without anyone knowing.

Practice

Step 1

Notice and acknowledge, "This hurts!" or "I'm struggling right now."

Step 2

Connect with other people who are suffering. We all experience challenges at some point. Experiment to find a phrase that resonates with you, for example, "We all struggle" or "This is what it is to be human."

Step 3

Offer yourself some kindness by repeating a phrase such as, "May I give myself what I need." It's fine to adapt and edit the words to whatever feels nurturing to you.

When you repeat the phrases silently to yourself, let them resonate in the body. If you feel comfortable doing so, you can place a hand over your heart.

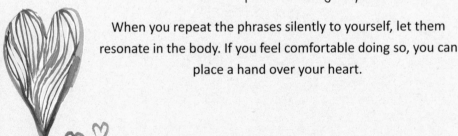

smile a little smile

When we are anxious or stressed, we tense up—often in the shoulders, the jaw, or around the forehead. There is a sense of tightening.

We can practice cultivating the opposite by softening inside. Imagine you are smiling inside. The lips soften, the throat opens, and there is a sense of release.

You can take this further by intentionally making eye contact and smiling at people you meet.

Can you smile inside today?

REMEMBER...
BE *curious*,
BE *kind*,
AND LET GO OF
expectations!

take a
challenge

As humans, we crave variety, and our desire to always be looking for something new and shiny often shows up in our practice. While there is a value in noticing this craving and sticking with our usual practice, we can also spice things up by setting ourselves a challenge. It is also a great way to weave our practice into our day.

ABOUT THE CHALLENGES

They are time-limited. It's easier to stay focused for a 3- or 5-day challenge rather than 30 days for example, so avoid setting yourself up to fail.

Certain parameters, boundaries, or guidelines are created to give structure. These may include specific tasks or practices to do on different days to help develop or deepen a practice.

There is an opportunity to reflect on what you notice.

You may do the challenges on your own or join up with others, and adapt them to suit your own circumstances.

tech detox challenge

Before doing this challenge, I recommend completing the practice on page 60. It's really helpful to have some insight into our habitual patterns of responding/reacting before we explore them further.

Having a break from technology can be really helpful. By technology I particularly mean smartphones with their 24/7 connectivity, but if you have identified other areas of technology where perhaps your relationship is a bit skewed you can do a similar type of challenge with them—for example, gaming or binge-watching box sets.

We are all guilty of sending an email when it would have been more appropriate to pick up the phone or have a face-to-face conversation. Can you think of an occasion when you wish you had done that?

We lose out on so much feedback when communicating via text or email. There's no opportunity to read body language or pick up a subtle nuances in the tone of voice. We miss things and can easily misinterpret the sender's intention. We all see the world through our own goggles that include filters depending on our mood or frame of mind. If we are feeling stressed or anxious, we are more likely to interpret something negatively than if we are feeling upbeat and positive.

A tech detox is a good choice if you feel that your relationship with your phone (or some aspect of it) has become a bit skewed and you are perhaps more of a slave to it (see box, opposite).

Some things to consider...

FOREWARN OR ENGAGE ANY INTERESTED PARTIES. Your children, partner, or boss isn't going to be impressed if they don't get a response to their messages and don't know why!

THERE'S SOLIDARITY IN NUMBERS. It can be really helpful to do this challenge with other people. If you are a parent concerned about your child's attachment to their phone, then this is a great opportunity to lead by example and do the challenge as a family.

SUPPORT YOURSELF FOR SUCCESS. For example, if you are guilty of checking your work emails/messages when you're at home (and there is no need to), turn off your phone and put it away if possible, or if you have your work emails on your personal phone take them off for the stipulated period.

WHAT DO YOU WANT TO FOCUS ON? Take some time to think about the scope of the challenge. See the boxes overleaf for some ideas. It's important to be realistic and better to set clear achievable boundaries initially and then expand them later if you wish, rather than set yourself up to fail by being too ambitious.

Consider what you want to include in the challenge:

Keeping office hours (work)

Social media usage

Email (work and/or personal)

Vacation time

Weekends

When do you find other people's use of phones most annoying? Use that as a starting point.

At mealtimes

During meetings

On the school run

At bedtimes

When someone could just as easily speak to you rather than send a text

It's helpful to set very clear boundaries about start and finish times and what is and is not included in the challenge (and remember, it's your choice).

THE CHALLENGE
Step 1: Record Your Challenge

Include any specifics about the challenge. Writing down clear intentions
and guidelines will help support you in your challenge.

DATE: DURATION:

....

....

....

....

....

Step 2: Reflect During The Challenge

What do you notice during the period of abstinence? Notice
what is arising in the HEAD, HEART, and BODY. If the challenge is going
on for a period of time (eg mealtimes for a week), record
any observations periodically.

....

....

....

....

....

....

....

....

....

Step 3: Reflect At The Conclusion Of The Challenge

What did you notice overall? Any surprises? Include any comments or observations from anyone else in the challenge. Be as specific as you can.

....

....

....

....

....

....

....

Write down any observations anyone not involved in the challenge noticed (for example your friends, family members, or co-workers).

....

....

....

....

....

....

....

....

Step 4: Takeaways

What learning would you like to take away from this?

....

....

....

....

....

....

....

What action step if any, would you like to implement? (Be as specific as you can. For example, you might decide that all future family mealtimes will be phone free. Or you may decide to extend the challenge to have an entire phone-free day... Be as creative as you can.)

....

....

....

....

....

....

....

....

5 days 5 senses challenge

You'll explore a different sense each day—intentionally looking at what arises and in particular whether you like the experience or not. You don't need to make any special preparations.

Set an intention each day to pay attention to the specific sense. You will forget, but any time you remember, see if you can connect with that sense in that moment.

The challenge is about exploring and discovering how you relate to your experience. You may like parts of it and you may dislike others or get bored by it. That's okay—it's all feedback.

Perhaps you have a long-standing belief that you don't like something. You may want to observe how you respond to it—not with the intention of liking it but as an opportunity to explore that resistance.

When you are focusing on the sensory experience, tune into the Head, Heart, and Body (see page 14) and see what you notice. Reflect on your experience during and at the end of each day— bringing to mind what you observed, if anything.

It's okay if you find yourself noticing senses from a previous day.

Remember we are not THINKING about the sense—we are connecting with the FELT EXPERIENCE of it.

You may want to pay attention to one thing you LOVE, one thing you DISLIKE, and one thing you are NEUTRAL about.

DAY 1: TASTE

WHAT DID YOU NOTICE?

Our memory affects our taste so if we recall a positive memory
about a particular food as we are eating, we will enjoy it more.
By paying attention to great tastes, we are then banking them
in our long-term memory.

DAY 2: TOUCH

WHAT DID YOU NOTICE?

....

....

....

....

....

....

....

....

....

....

....

....

....

....

....

....

....

Touching—hugging, stroking, rubbing, massaging—can be very soothing
as the body releases endorphins and levels of cortisol, the stress
hormone, are reduced. You can also benefit from massaging cream
onto your own skin or spending some time stroking a pet.

DAY 3: SIGHT

WHAT DID YOU NOTICE?

What do you turn away from? We can unconsciously shift our view from something that makes us uncomfortable—the homeless woman on the street or the starving child on the TV news. If you actually look and see what is there, what do you notice?

DAY 4: SOUND

WHAT DID YOU NOTICE?

Pay attention to whether you judge something as sound or noise.
How does the body respond in terms of physical sensations?
What narrative do you notice in your thoughts?

DAY 5: SMELL

WHAT DID YOU NOTICE?

....

....

....

....

....

....

....

....

....

....

....

....

....

....

....

....

....

....

80 percent of what we experience as taste is actually smell. Like
taste, there are strong associations between smell and memory.
What memories do you associate with particular scents?

do something
different challenge

When we visit somewhere new, we are usually alert—paying attention to the surroundings and smells—and we are more likely to experiment and try new things.

At home, we can get caught up in routines—we follow familiar paths and routes; we "know" the neighborhood so we don't actually look around; we tune out from directly experiencing and are more likely to get caught up in thinking. We can also get stuck in doing things a certain way because that's how they've always been done.

This challenge is designed to encourage you to break out from your routines and habitual patterns. Cultivating the ability to respond to the unexpected builds our emotional resilience and reawakens curiosity.

This is a five-day challenge but you could make it shorter or longer.

Each day, explore how many things you can do differently.

To begin with, you may struggle to find things, but be as creative as you can with small choices as well as the bigger ones.

It's about discovery and exploration—what you notice about your response to breaking free of habitual patterns. Sometimes it may be exciting and pleasurable, other times it might feel quite comfortable.

What do you learn about yourself, your environment, and other people?

DAY 1

MAYBE...

Take a different route.

Choose a
different seat.

DAY 2

MAYBE...

Eat something different.

Drink something different—a different brand, flavor, topping.

DAY 3

MAYBE...

If you usually eat your lunch indoors, try going outside (or vice versa).

If you usually read a book or listen to music on your commute, what happens if you simply sit with the experience without any distraction?

DAY 4

MAYBE...

Make eye contact
with people.

Wear a color or
pattern you would
normally avoid.

DAY 5

MAYBE...

Shake up your
timetable—go to the
shops or gym at a
different time to usual,
leave the house a few
minutes earlier or later...

SETTING YOURSELF
a goal
TO DO SOMETHING OVER
A *specific period* OF TIME
CAN *really focus*
YOUR PRACTICE.

THE BOUNDARIES SUPPORT
your intention
AND HELP YOU REMEMBER
TO DO THE PRACTICES.

noticing what we have: a 10-day challenge

We can waste time focusing on what we don't have—perhaps a physical attribute or a skill, a level of income, or the right partner... the list goes on. This dissatisfaction can create unhappiness for us, so it makes sense that focusing on what we do have will make us feel better.

The invitation here is to start noticing and acknowledging what you have. It might be personal qualities, people you are lucky enough to have in your life, interests, skills, your environment, and so on.

You can do this practice at bedtime when you take a moment to reflect back on your day but you could also do it any other time.

Remember:

Be as specific as you can about what it is you appreciate.

Try not to repeat things.

Don't get hung up on words like gratitude and adapt to what resonates with you.

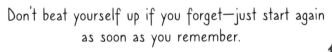

Don't beat yourself up if you forget—just start again as soon as you remember.

This is a great challenge to do with children.

DAYS 1-5

Name five things you appreciate or are grateful for in your life.
This might be people, actions, the environment, abilities, and so on.
Be as specific as you can be. Count them off on one hand. Try to
come up with different things each day.

DAYS 6-10

Up the ante and name 10 things you appreciate or are grateful for.
Be as creative as you can!

Keep this as simple as possible, so no need to write down
something each day but you might want to reflect what
you notice at the start, middle, and end of the
challenge. How do you feel about yourself, your life,
and the people around you?

REFLECTION

AT THE START

DAY 5

DAY 10

a personal retreat

How often do you have the opportunity to remove yourself from your everyday obligations and distractions? The endless to-do lists, the lure of the smartphone, Netflix, and work and family can all fill up our time. We all need some space and time to recharge and connect with ourselves. This challenge is for you to find a way to create that space for yourself. Start with an hour or two, but ideally set aside a half day. However, anything is better than nothing.

Do this on your own to avoid temptations of chatting. However, you could do it with a like-minded friend if you both commit to being silent—although you might want a period of reflection at the end.

Make a commitment to turn off your phone and other tech distractions. You can forewarn anyone who might need to know.

Think about where you want to be. You may want to stay at home or perhaps go away somewhere.

Although I'd encourage you to be in silence and avoid any unnecessary talking, it can be interesting to be in silence in a busy place, so perhaps mix quiet environments with noisier ones.

Plan what you are going to do (see page 124 for some ideas), but be willing to set that plan aside. You might sit in meditation for short periods and break this up with movement practices such as walking, yoga, and qigong. Or your retreat may be purely informal practices done in silence—many traditional retreats view daily activities such as cooking, cleaning, and gardening as important a practice as sitting in meditation. Or you can mix both formal and informal.

Journaling your experience can be interesting and you can make that one of the practices you do in between others.

Gather some resources, such as a variety of guided meditations to listen to. Vary practices and include some you might not usually do.

Your senses may become heightened so herbal teas and tasty snacks can increase the sensory experience.

If you are at home, you may want to light some scented candles and make a comfortable and inviting space, gathering any mats, props, or pillows you need if you are sitting on the floor or for the movement practices

REMEMBER, WE ARE *not chasing* A PARTICULAR EXPERIENCE.

YOU MAY EXPERIENCE PERIODS OF *calm* AND *peace*, BUT YOU ARE JUST AS LIKELY TO BE *bored, restless,* AND *sleepy!*

POSSIBLE PLAN FOR A HALF DAY

5 minutes Sit, allowing yourself to settle and check in with how you are feeling. Notice any expectations or emotions that may be present.

15 minutes Journal, or reflect with another, about your expectations for the day. Then go into silence if you are with someone else.

20 minutes Body scan meditation.

10 minutes Movement meditation such as walking, stretching, yoga, and qigong.

10 minutes Sitting practice.

10 minutes Movement meditation such as walking, stretching, yoga, and qigong.

15 minutes Sitting practice.

15 minutes Journal.

30 minutes Informal practice such as cooking, cleaning, gardening.

10 minutes Sitting practice.

40 minutes Lunch—mindful eating

5 minutes Sit, allowing yourself to settle and check in with how you are feeling. Notice any expectations or emotions that may be present.

15 minutes Reflection/journal about the experience.

Check out the resources on page 143 for a variety of free guided downloads for different sitting, lying down, and movement practices that you could use.

REFLECTION

just one thing: a 21-day challenge

This challenge brings together many of the practices in this book. Make an intention to focus on just one thing each day for 21 days. Every day you will move on to a different activity .

Start at Day I and work through the list. Left to choose, we can sometimes avoid those that don't appeal to us, but which might be rich in learning. However, always take care of yourself and don't do anything that isn't right for you.

Let go of any expectations. Regard it as an experiment. You may not enjoy or like some of the activities and that's okay.

Try to do the practice several times in the day if possible.

Notice what comes up when you do it. How does it make you feel? What do you observe in the head (thoughts), heart (emotions), and body (physical sensations)? Reflect on what you notice.

Don't give yourself a hard time if you forget or skip a day. Just start again from where you left off as soon as you remember.

Schedule

Tagging an activity to your existing routine will help jog a mental prompt so, before you start, make an intention to do the practice at three specific times, for example mealtimes. You may forget but the act of scheduling means at some point you will remember, and if possible do the practice then or as soon as you can.

Remember, it's not about having to like the activity.

☐ DAY 1 Pause for three: take three conscious breaths throughout your day.

....

....

....

....

☐ DAY 2 Imagine you are breathing through your feet on the floor for a few breaths. Try it when standing, sitting, and in public spaces.

....

....

....

....

☐ DAY 3 Tune into touch points—where your body is in contact with another surface, such as a seat, the floor, another part of the body, clothing, a person, an object... How many different touch points can you notice through the day?

....

....

....

....

....

No need to judge the judging mind.

☐ DAY 4 Taste one thing you would not usually choose (as long as it's safe for you), because "I don't eat XYZ." Imagine you've never had it before—what do you notice in terms of thoughts, physical sensations, and emotions? Remember, it's not about liking it.

☐ DAY 5 Tune into sounds through the day. Notice how you relate to them—which ones do you soften into and which do you tense up around? What stories are you telling yourself about them?

☐ DAY 6 Explore the sense of touch. Observe different surfaces—play with different ways you can explore them.

☐ DAY 7 Stop and see something you normally turn away from. Pause and tune into what is arising in the body, noticing emotions and the story unfolding in your mind.

....

....

....

....

☐ DAY 8 Stop and look at something that catches your eye. Look carefully and notice how it affects you physically, as well as your mood.

....

....

....

....

☐ DAY 9 Focus on doing just one thing at a time. Do your best to give your full attention to every person and activity today.

....

....

....

....

Be aware of the internal critical voice—the thoughts are real but they are not true!

☐ DAY 10 Carry out random acts of kindness. Open a door for someone, give up your seat, let someone take your parking space... Be creative.

....

....

....

☐ DAY 11 What is your relationship with your smartphone? Notice how often you check it. How do these interactions make you feel?

....

....

....

Congratulations—you are over halfway through the challenge!

☐ DAY 12 Smile and make eye contact with others.

....

....

....

☐ DAY 13 Be curious about cravings, noticing when you reach for that cookie, chocolate, or drink. Can you pause and tune into the head, heart, and body? If you choose to take the item, do so with awareness.

....

....

Touch in to your head, heart, and body.

....

....

☐ DAY 14 Pick a color such as red and use that as your marker—and every time you see it, pause and breathe for three rounds.

....

....

....

....

☐ DAY 15 Notice temperature. Every time you have a drink, take a moment to feel the heat or cold on your hands. Experience how it feels externally and then internally as you drink it.

....

....

....

....

☐ DAY 16 Notice the judging mind: how you talk to yourself and how you judge others. Are you kind or hard on yourself?

....

....

....

....

Notice how you relate to your experience—the liking or not liking—and how it feels physically in the body.

☐ DAY 17 Smile inside. What do you notice?

....

....

....

☐ DAY 18 Practice curiosity. Be curious about everything—ask questions without expecting a particular answer. Be a beginner!

....

....

....

☐ DAY 19 Tune in to the body throughout the day. Notice both internal and external sensations—which ones you like and those you don't.

....

....

....

☐ DAY 20 Be curious about boredom. Notice when you are bored. What do you do? Where does your mind go? Become interested in it?

....

....

....

....

☐ DAY 21 Do at least one thing you would usually avoid. It may be something you've been putting off or something you don't like doing. Do it with awareness. What do you notice?

....

....

....

....

Congratulations!

CHOOSE THREE THINGS YOU WOULD LIKE TO CONTINUE TO
PRACTICE EACH DAY AND WRITE THEM DOWN HERE:

1. ....

2. ....

3. ....

DATE FOR REVIEW:

....

my mindfulness challenge

Why don't you set yourself your own mindfulness challenge? Choose something you would like to explore—be as specific as you can be. Decide on the scope of the challenge—how often and for how long. Reflect on what you notice as you go along and then at the end of the challenge when you look back.

DESCRIPTION AND INTENTION:

DURATION:

WHAT DO YOU NOTICE?

my favorite mindfulness practices

Make a list of those practices you come back to time and time again. Perhaps you do them in response to specific situations or moods and, if so, make a note of that, too. When you are feeling stuck, revisit the list and choose one to do, without any expectations of it changing the way you feel.

☐

☐

☐

☐

☐

☐

☐

☐

my least favorite mindfulness practices

Make a list of those practices you avoid. They might be different meditations or informal practices. Notice if there are any specific reasons you are aware of that discourage you from doing them. From time to time, pick something from the list and explore how your attitude is—practice beginner's mind, letting go of expectations, and being curious about what you notice. It is not about learning to like a practice but simply about reminding ourselves that our experience changes at different times and we never know how we might respond. Experiment and see for yourself!

podcasts I want to listen to

Podcasts are a great way to be inspired, whether you are on the move or at home. Many podcasts are interview-based and so allow you to hear your favorite author or teacher speak about the subject—and often you can ask questions, too.

books I want to read

Reading can be a great way to stimulate and motivate your practice. Some of my favorite authors are Jon Kabat-Zinn, Jack Kornfield, Sharon Salzberg, Pema Chödrön, Christopher Germer, Kristin Neff, Thich Nhat Hanh, and Tara Brach. Make a note of your favorites here and any particular titles you want to read.

FURTHER REFLECTIONS

my lists

Here you can keep notes of your favorite resources that will inform and strengthen your practice.

RESOURCES

There are many guided meditation practices and teachings online. Here are a few of the best.

Centre for Mindfulness Research and Practice (CMRP), Bangor University

This website has a wide range of guided meditations of varying lengths from CMRP teachers. They include core practices such as the body scan, a variety of sitting practices, including the Mountain Meditation, movement practices, and mindful yoga and walking. There are also some in the Welsh language.

https://www.bangor.ac.uk/mindfulness/audio/index.php.en

Center for Mindful Self-Compassion

Christopher Germer and Kristin Neff co-founded the Center for Mindful Self-Compassion and developed the Mindful Self-Compassion course. A variety of compassion-focused practices are available to download from this website.

www.self-compassion.org

Oxford Mindfulness Centre

The Oxford Mindfulness Centre has launched a free app to support students taking its Mindfulness-Based Cognitive Therapy (MBCT) course, which features a variety of guided practices.

www.oxfordmindfulness.org

Tara Brach

Meditation teacher and author provides guided practice and resources.

www.tarabrach.com/guided-meditations/

University of California, Los Angeles (UCLA) Mindful Awareness Research Center

Log on for guided meditations in English and Spanish.

https://www.uclahealth.org/marc/body.cfm?id=22&iirf_redirect=1

The UC San Diego Center for Mindfulness

Guided meditations and guided audio and video of mindful yoga practices.

https://health.ucsd.edu/specialties/mindfulness/programs/mbsr/Pages/audio.aspx

Practice for Living

This is an online membership run by Anna Black to help people strengthen and deepen their practice, and weave mindfulness throughout their day. Download the free Practice for Living app for free practices and resources.

https://www.practiceforliving.com

Anna's main website is www.mindfulness-meditation-now.com

BIBLIOGRAPHY

There are many books that have fed and informed my practice, and it would be impossible to list them all, but here are a few favorites:

Full Catastrophe Living, Jon Kabat-Zinn (Piatkus, 2013)

Wherever You Go, There You Are, Jon Kabat-Zinn (Piatkus, 2004)

Buddha's Brain: The Practical Neuroscience of Happiness, Love, and Wisdom, Rick Hanson (New Harbinger, 2009)

A Path with Heart, Jack Kornfield (Rider, 2002)

The Art of Forgiveness, LovingKindness and Peace, Jack Kornfield (Bantam, 2002)

The Miracle of Mindfulness, Thich Nhat Hanh (Rider, 2008)

The Mindful Path to Self-Compassion, Christopher Germer (Guilford Press, 2009)

Self Compassion, Kristin Neff (Yellow Kite 2011)

Radical Acceptance, Tara Brach (Rider, 2003)

When Things Fall Apart, Pema Chödrön (Element Books, 2007)

Mindfulness in 8 Weeks, Michael Chaskalson (Harper Thorsons, 2014)

Mindfulness: a practical guide to finding peace in a frantic world, Mark Williams and Dr Danny Penman (Piatkus, 2011)

Loving-Kindness: The Revolutionary Art of Happiness, Sharon Salzberg (Shambhala Publications, 2002)